6.1/1.0

Rick Riordan

Anita Yasuda

www.av2books.com

AV² provides enriched content that supplements and complements this book. Weigl's AV² books strive to create inspired learning and engage young minds in a total learning experience.

Your AV² Media Enhanced books come alive with...

Audio
Listen to sections of the book read aloud.

Key Words
Study vocabulary, and complete a matching word activity.

Video
Watch informative video clips.

Quizzes
Test your knowledge.

Go to **www.av2books.com**, and enter this book's unique code.

BOOK CODE

N 5 7 3 3 7 4

Embedded Weblinks
Gain additional information for research.

Slide Show
View images and captions, and prepare a presentation.

AV² by Weigl brings you media enhanced books that support active learning.

Try This!
Complete activities and hands-on experiments.

... and much, much more!

Published by AV² by Weigl
350 5th Avenue, 59th Floor
New York, NY 10118

Website: www.weigl.com   www.av2books.com

Library of Congress Cataloging-in-Publication Data

Yasuda, Anita.
 Rick Riordan / Anita Yasuda.
     pages cm. -- (Remarkable Writers)
 Includes index.
 Summary: "Part of a biography series that profiles children's authors of the twentieth century. Explores the life of Rick Riordan and his most popular books, with additional facts provided through a timeline, awards, and fan information. Includes photographs, creative writing tips, and instruction on how to write a biography report. Intended for fourth to sixth grade students"--Provided by publisher.
 ISBN 978-1-62127-403-2 (hardcover : alk. paper) -- ISBN 978-1-62127-409-4 (softcover : alk. paper)
 1. Riordan, Rick--Juvenile literature. 2. Authors, American--20th century--Biography--Juvenile literature. 3. Children's literature--Authorship--Juvenile literature. I. Title.
 PS3568.I5866Z96 2013
 813'.54--dc23
 [B]
                              2012041281

Printed in the United States of America, in North Mankato, Minnesota
1 2 3 4 5 6 7 8 9 0 17 16 15 14 13

012013
WEP301112

Senior Editor: Heather Kissock
Design: Terry Paulhus

Weigl acknowledges Getty Images as its primary photo supplier for this title.

Contents

Introducing
Rick Riordan

Rick Riordan is an award-winning author of novels for adults and children. His two most popular children's series, Percy Jackson & the Olympians and The Kane Chronicles, have earned Rick fans all over the world. Rick Riordan's novels have placed him on the #1 *New York Times* Best Sellers list. His work has won him many awards. In 2011, the Children's Choice Book Awards named Rick its Author of the Year.

Ever since he was young, Rick has enjoyed reading stories based on **mythology**. He was especially interested in the myths of ancient Greece. Myths have characters that have supernatural powers. They throw thunderbolts and cause storms to occur. Rick was attracted to the drama and fantasy of these stories.

Rick Riordan attends events to meet his fans. He measures his success on the feedback he receives from his readers and their parents.

When he was older and had children of his own, Rick liked to tell myths as bedtime stories. However, he eventually ran out of myths to tell. When this happened, he began creating his own stories based on mythical characters. These stories later became published books. Today, Rick's books entertain children of all ages, while also teaching them about the history and myths of ancient **civilizations**.

In 2010, Rick's novel *Percy Jackson & the Olympians: The Lightning Thief* was released as a movie. Logan Lerman played the role of Percy.

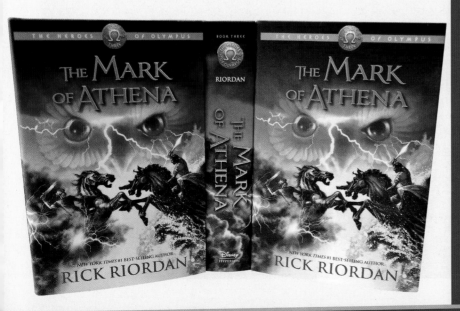

Writing A Biography

Writers are often inspired to record the stories of people who lead interesting lives. The story of another person's life is called a biography. A biography can tell the story of any person, from authors such as Rick Riordan, to inventors, presidents, and sports stars.

When writing a biography, authors must first collect information about their subject. This information may come from a book about the person's life, a news article about one of his or her accomplishments, or a review of his or her work. Libraries and the internet will have much of this information. Most biographers will also interview their subjects. Personal accounts provide a great deal of information and a unique point of view. When some basic details about the person's life have been collected, it is time to begin writing a biography.

As you read about Rick Riordan, you will be introduced to the important parts of a biography. Use these tips and the examples provided to learn how to write about an author or any other remarkable person.

Early Life

Rick Riordan was born on June 5, 1964. He grew up in San Antonio, Texas. Rick's parents were both teachers. His father, Rick Riordan, Sr., was a **vocational** teacher. Rick's mother, Lyn Belisle, taught English, art, and **graphic design**.

"Having parents who read is critical, because modeling that behavior will show children that reading is an important and enjoyable part of family life." —*Rick Riordan*

Rick grew up in a loving and creative home. His mother was a writer, artist, and musician who allowed Rick to discover his own interests. Whenever Rick complained of being bored, his mother encouraged him to think of different activities he might enjoy doing. She wanted Rick to find ways to entertain himself. This gave Rick the opportunity to daydream and create his own fantasy worlds.

San Antonio is located in south-central Texas. It has a population of about 1.3 million, making it the seventh most populous city in the United States.

Rick's father was also artistic. He liked to write poetry and make pottery. He often took Rick along with him to his pottery class. Rick would make dinosaur sculptures while his father worked on his pottery. They would then try to sell their creations.

At night, Rick's father would read bedtime stories to his son. He was a storyteller who instilled in Rick a love for reading. Many of Rick's favorite stories came from a book called *Tales of the Western World*. Rick enjoyed listening to his father read the book's American Indian myths and American **folktales**.

Rick remembers his father sharing Paul Bunyan stories with him. These classic American folktales describe the adventures of a giant lumberjack named Paul and his animal friend Babe the Blue Ox.

A person's early years have a strong influence on his or her future. Parents, teachers, and friends can have a large impact on how a person thinks, feels, and behaves. These effects are strong enough to last throughout childhood, and often a person's lifetime.

In order to write about a person's early life, biographers must find answers to the following questions.

1 Where and when was the person born?

2 What is known about the person's family and friends?

3 Did the person grow up in unusual circumstances?

Growing Up

Rick was a quiet child. He liked to spend his time building toys he could play with. Rick could often be found playing with his Lego set or putting a toy robot together. Rick also liked going to school. He often thought that he could explain the lesson just as well as the teacher did.

"I can't remember a time when I wasn't interested in mythology…"
—*Rick Riordan*

Rick was not a keen reader as a child, however. He enjoyed the stories his parents read to him at home, but did not like the books he had to read at school. Rick could not relate to the stories.

It was only when Rick was about 12 years of age that he began to enjoy reading. This is when his eighth grade English teacher, Mrs. Pabst, became aware of Rick's dislike of the school's reading list. Mrs. Pabst began to look for books that might appeal to the reluctant reader. When she handed Rick a set of fantasy novels, she introduced Rick to a lifelong love of reading.

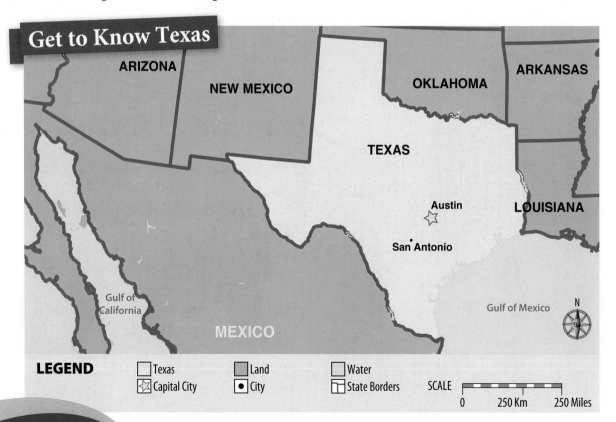

Get to Know Texas

ARIZONA

NEW MEXICO

OKLAHOMA

ARKANSAS

TEXAS

Austin

LOUISIANA

San Antonio

Gulf of California

Gulf of Mexico

N

MEXICO

LEGEND

☐ Texas ☐ Land ☐ Water

⬡ Capital City ● City ⊞ State Borders

SCALE

0   250 Km   250 Miles

Books such as J. R. R. Tolkien's series The Lord of The Rings captivated him. After Mrs. Pabst told Rick that the Tolkien books were inspired by **Norse** mythology, he wanted to find out more and studied books on this topic. As he learned more about the fantasy **genre**, Rick became interested in creating stories similar to those he was reading.

Rick began writing **short stories**. He even tried to have his work published. Rick was only 12 years old when he sent his first short story to *Isaac Asimov's Science Fiction Magazine*. Isaac Asimov was an award-winning science fiction author. Even though the story was not accepted for publication, Rick enjoyed the writing process. He continued to write and, a few years later, won third prize in a **University Interscholastic League** (UIL) writing contest.

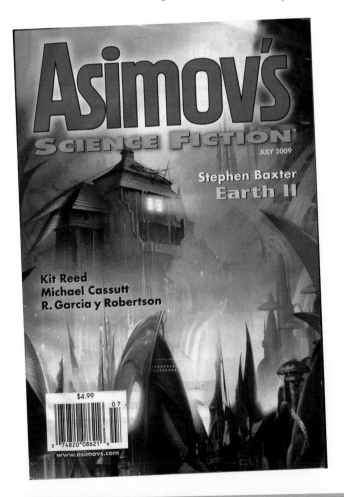

Writing About
Growing Up

Some people know what they want to achieve in life from a very young age. Others do not decide until much later. In any case, it is important for biographers to discuss when and how their subjects make these decisions. Using the information they collect, biographers try to answer the following questions about their subjects' paths in life.

1 Who had the most influence on the person?

2 Did he or she receive assistance from others?

3 Did the person have a positive attitude?

📖 *Isaac Asimov's Science Fiction Magazine* was started in 1977. Initially a quarterly magazine, it eventually became a monthly digest. In 1992, the magazine's name was shortened to *Asimov's Science Fiction*.

Developing Skills

Although Rick now enjoyed writing, he also developed an interest in music. After high school, Rick thought that he might like to be a **professional** musician. He enjoyed playing the guitar and had dreams of becoming a rock star. Rick decided to attend North Texas State, now known as the University of North Texas, to pursue a career in music. The university has one of the largest collections of music in the United States. It was also the first university in the world to offer a degree in jazz.

> "A good book always keeps you asking questions, and makes you keep turning pages so you can find out the answers." —*Rick Riordan*

However, despite his interest in music, his time at the university made him realize how important **literature** was to him. He loved his English classes because they introduced him to books that he had never read in high school. He began to think about becoming an English teacher. He liked the idea of being able to read and discuss books for a living.

Rick played guitar throughout his school years. This skill eventually helped him become the music director at a summer camp. He later drew on his camp experiences when writing the Percy Jackson series.

Rick decided to transfer to the University of Texas at Austin. Here, he began working towards a degree in English and history. Rick also continued to develop his own writing. He was able to get two of his short stories published in the university's literary magazine.

Rick graduated from university in 1986. Two years later, he received his teaching certificate. He also married. He and his wife Becky then moved to San Francisco, California, where Rick began studying for a degree in English and **Medieval** Studies. He later accepted a teaching position at a local school. For the next few years, Rick taught English and history to middle school students. All the while, he continued to write, focusing his attention on mysteries.

San Francisco is located on the west coast of the United States. It is considered the financial and cultural center of northern California.

Writing About Developing Skills

Every remarkable person has skills and traits that make him or her noteworthy. Some people have natural talent, while others practice diligently. For most, it is a combination of the two. One of the most important things that a biographer can do is to tell the story of how the subject developed his or her talents.

1 What was the person's education?

2 What was the person's first job or work experience?

3 What obstacles did the person overcome?

Timeline of Rick Riordan

1964
Rick Riordan is born in San Antonio, Texas, on June 5.

1986
Rick graduates from the University of Texas at Austin with a degree in English and history.

1988
Rick receives his teaching certificate. Soon after, he and his wife move to San Francisco, California, where he continues his education.

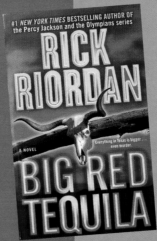

1997
Rick's debut novel, a mystery for adults called *Big Red Tequila*, is published. The book wins the 1997 Anthony Award for Best Original Paperback.

1990
Rick begins teaching at a middle school in the San Francisco Bay area.

1998

Rick and his family move to San Antonio, Texas.

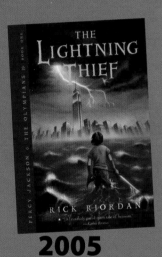

2005

Rick's first novel for young adults called *Percy Jackson & the Olympians: The Lightning Thief* is published.

2007

Rick's third book in the Percy Jackson series, *The Titan's Curse,* becomes number one on the *New York Times* children's series bestseller list.

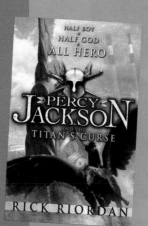

2011

Rick is named Author of the Year by the Children's Book Council.

2010

The movie *Percy Jackson & the Olympians: The Lightning Thief* is released. It is **nominated** for several MTV Movie and Teen Choice awards.

Early Achievements

Rick enjoyed teaching in the San Francisco Bay area. He loved getting to know his students and seeing them mature. He also enjoyed teaching them about literature, especially mythology. Rick worked hard as a teacher and expected his students to be excited about learning. He wanted them to leave his room wanting to read more, not less.

"...I often asked teachers what I should write about, only to be given that old axiom, 'Write about what you know.' I hated that, since I didn't know anything. It was only after moving away from San Antonio that I realized what a unique place it was."—*Rick Riordan*

Even though he was teaching all day and going to school himself, Rick still found time to write short stories. He often submitted them to magazine publishers to see if they would publish them. He was rewarded in 1998, when the *Mary Higgins Clark Mystery Magazine* published his short story 'A Small Silver Gun.' Some of Rick's other stories were then published in *Ellery Queen's Mystery Magazine*. This is the oldest and longest-running short story mystery magazine in the world.

Rick looks to other mystery writers for inspiration. He especially likes the works of Dashiell Hammett.

Rick liked living in San Francisco, but there were times when he missed San Antonio. In order to feel closer to home, he decided to write a book based in his hometown. *Big Red Tequila* follows a private detective called Tres Navarre as he tries to solve a mystery in San Antonio.

Bantam Books published *Big Red Tequila* in 1997. The book won several literary awards for achievement in mystery fiction, including the Anthony Award for best original paperback and the Shamus award for best first private investigator novel. A year later, *The Widower's Two-Step*, a **sequel** to *Big Red Tequila*, was released. Rick was on his way to becoming a successful author.

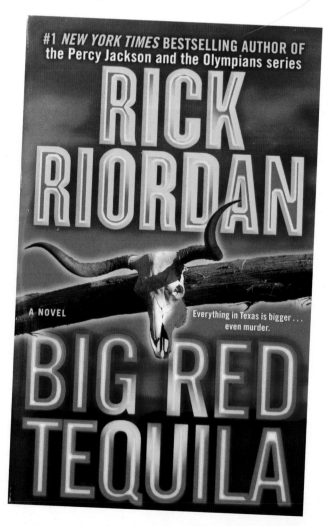

#1 *NEW YORK TIMES* BESTSELLING AUTHOR OF
the Percy Jackson and the Olympians series

RICK RIORDAN

A NOVEL

Everything in Texas is bigger …
even murder.

BIG RED TEQUILA

Writing About

Early Achievements

No two people take the same path to success. Some people work very hard for a long time before achieving their goals. Others may take advantage of a fortunate turn of events. Biographers must make special note of the traits and qualities that allow their subjects to succeed.

1 What was the person's most important early success?

2 What processes does the person use in his or her work?

3 Which of the person's traits were most helpful in his or her work?

The manuscript for *Big Red Tequila* was finished in 1994, but was rejected by many agents and publishers. It took three more years before it would become a published book.

Tricks of the Trade

Writing a story or a poem can be challenging, but it can also be very rewarding. Some writers have trouble coming up with ideas, while others have so many ideas that they do not know where to start. Rick Riordan has special writing habits that young writers can follow to develop their own ideas and stories.

Find Inspiration

Good writers are excited about their subjects. Think about what excites or interests you. It could be a person, an activity, a place, or a dream you have had. Rick was inspired by his own interest in mythology to create new mythological characters and exciting adventures.

Write, Write, Write

Sometimes, the easiest way to finish a poem or a story is to write as much as possible in a first **draft**. This way, a writer can get all of his or

her ideas down on paper. Very few writers have ever produced a great story in just one draft. Instead, they review their first draft to see which parts to keep and what needs to be **revised**. When Rick first started writing stories, he showed his work to his students. They gave him feedback and helped him decide which parts of the story worked well and which parts needed to be changed.

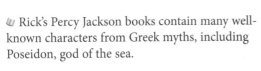 Rick's Percy Jackson books contain many well-known characters from Greek myths, including Poseidon, god of the sea.

The Creative Process

Most writers have different opinions about when is the best time to write. Some work best late at night when everyone else is asleep. Others claim that they are most productive early in the morning. Rick does not have a set writing schedule. Usually, he writes early in the morning or late at night when the house is quiet. Often, his writing time is scheduled in between family activities and business.

"...I always imagine myself telling the story in front of my own classroom. I try to fashion a story that works well read aloud, that will keep the attention of a young audience." —*Rick Riordan*

It Takes Dedication

Writing takes **dedication** and **discipline**. Rick worked for 15 years as a teacher and wrote stories in his spare time. It took months for him to finish a book. Rick advises aspiring writers to keep writing their stories, even if they feel they need more time to write the story properly. He believes that people who really want to write will always find the time. Rick also encourages writers to never give up. They need to keep trying until they find the story that they were truly meant to tell.

When promoting his books, Rick often takes the time to advise aspiring writers on the creative process.

Remarkable Books

Although he has written books for adults, Rick Riordan enjoys writing for children. He is best known for his novels for young adults. His fantasy adventure books, including the Percy Jackson & the Olympians series, appeal to readers of all ages.

The Lightning Thief

Rick Riordan's first book tells the story of 12-year-old Percy Jackson. After accidentally vaporizing his math teacher, Percy discovers that he is half human and half god. His father is Poseidon, god of the sea. Percy is sent to Camp Half-Blood, where he meets other **demigod** children. While at the camp, he discovers that the thunderbolt of Zeus has been stolen. Percy and his new friends, Grover and Annabeth, set out on a quest to recover the missing thunderbolt.

AWARDS
The Lightning Thief
2005 *New York Times* Notable Book
2005 ALA Notable Book
2006 Red House Children's Book Award Winner

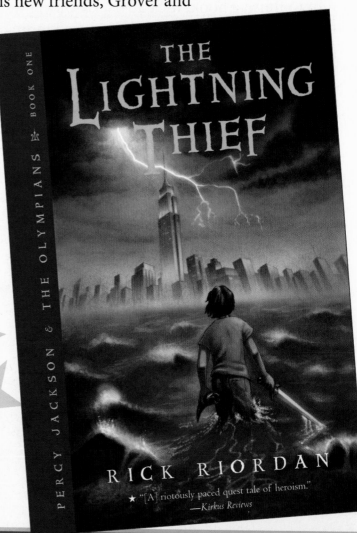

The Sea of Monsters

In *The Sea of Monsters*, the second book in the Percy Jackson series, Percy and his friends must find the **Golden Fleece** in order to save Camp Half-Blood from monsters. During his quest, Percy has many exciting adventures. He sails into the dreaded Sea of Monsters, rescues his friend Grover from the Cyclops's island, and saves Annabeth from drowning. Percy also discovers a family secret, which makes him wonder if being the son of Poseidon is something to be proud of after all.

The Lost Hero

The Lost Hero is a book about the importance of friendship. It is part of Rick's Heroes of Olympus series. The main character in the series is Jason. When the story begins, Jason is sitting in a school bus. He has no idea who he is or where he is. Fortunately, other people on the bus know him and inform Jason that he is on a field trip to the Grand Canyon. When one of the other students on the bus turns into a storm spirit, Jason is thrust into the world of Greek and Roman gods. Along with his friends Piper and Leo, Jason sets out on journey to save Hera, queen of the gods.

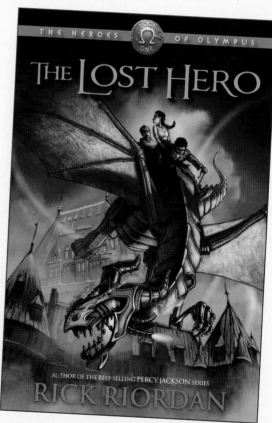

The Son of Neptune

The *Son of Neptune* is the second book in the Heroes of Olympus series. When Percy Jackson awakens from a long sleep, he finds that he has lost most of his memory. He can only remember his own name and that of his friend, Annabeth. Percy sets out on a mission for Ares, the leader of the Roman camp. Percy and his friends, Frank, Reyna, and Hazel, travel to Alaska on a dangerous quest to free Thanatos, the god of death, and help save the world from Gaea, the earth goddess.

The Maze of Bones

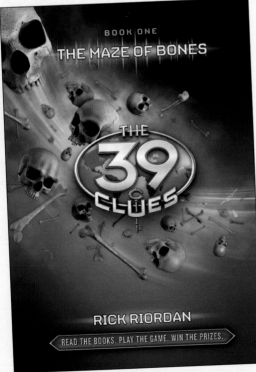

The Maze of Bones is the first book in The 39 Clues series. When Dan and Amy Cahill's grandmother dies, her will reveals a family secret. Dan and Amy learn that they are part of the most important family in the world. They are given the choice to either receive $1 million or go on a quest to find a priceless treasure. Dan and Amy decide to go on the quest. Their travels take them to Paris where they compete with others searching for the clues to an ancient mystery.

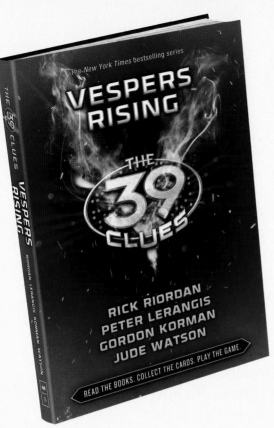

Vespers Rising

This action-packed book is part of The 39 Clues series. Rick Riordan, Gordon Korman, Peter Lerangis, and Jude Watson wrote the book together. Each author created his own story within the book. The reader is taken on a journey back in time to learn the origins of the Cahill family secret. Rick Riordan's story is about Gideon Cahill, the patriarch of the Cahill family, and how his family first became divided. The novel also explains the origin of the 39 clues that are the main theme of the series.

The Red Pyramid

The Red Pyramid is the first book in The Kane Chronicles series, featuring siblings Carter and Sadie Kane. Since their mother's death, Sadie has lived with her grandparents in London, while Carter has traveled the world with their father, an **Egyptologist**. On a visit to London, their father takes the children to the British Museum, where he summons Set, an ancient Egyptian god. In an exciting adventure, Carter and Sadie struggle to save their father. As they do so, they learn that they are descended from the most powerful magicians in ancient Egypt.

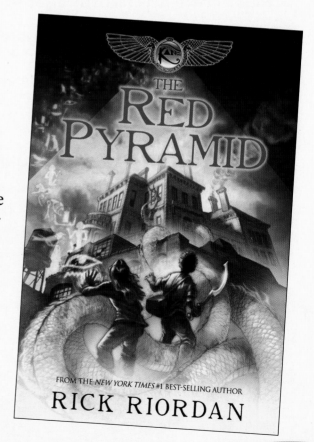

From Big Ideas to Books

Rick felt it was important to pass his love of reading on to his two sons, Patrick and Haley. Like his father, Haley loved to listen to bedtime stories. He especially liked Greek myths. One evening, Rick ran out of Greek myths to tell his son. Haley was disappointed and asked his father to create a new myth. In the course of three evenings, Rick created the character of Percy Jackson, who must go on a quest to recover the lightning bolt of Zeus. Haley loved the story. He suggested that Rick write a book about it.

> "It's not a bad thing to be different. Sometimes, it's the mark of being very, very talented. That's what Percy discovers about himself in *The Lightning Thief*."
> —*Rick Riordan*

Before long, Rick set to work at writing his first children's book. He decided to base the character of Percy Jackson on Haley. Percy and Haley both have **attention deficit hyperactivity disorder** (ADHD) and **dyslexia**.

While writing, Rick looked to his boys for guidance. He would read his **manuscript** aloud to his sons. If their interest began to waver, he would rewrite the text until it held their attention right to the end.

The Publishing Process

Publishing companies receive hundreds of manuscripts from authors each year. Only a few manuscripts become books. Publishers must be sure that a manuscript will sell many copies. As a result, publishers reject most of the manuscripts they receive. Once a manuscript has been accepted, it goes through

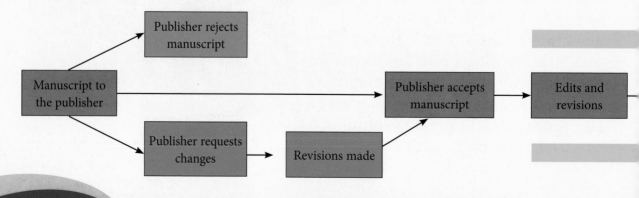

The Lightning Thief was published in 2005 and became an instant success. Rick continued the Percy Jackson series with four more books. Each went on to be a bestseller. The series has been published in more than 30 countries and has sold more than 20 million books worldwide.

In 2010, *The Lightning Thief* was developed into a movie. Starring Pierce Bronson and Uma Thurman, the movie made more than $225 million. The film was so well received that its producers decided to continue the series. Filming on the sequel, *The Sea of Monsters*, began in 2012.

Haley Riordan sometimes accompanies his father to writing events to talk about how he helped Rick develop the Percy Jackson books.

many stages before it is published. Often, authors change their work to follow an editor's suggestions. Once the book is published, some authors receive royalties. This is money based on book sales.

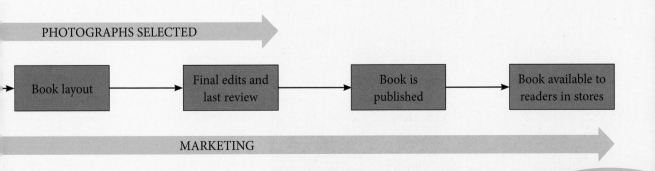

PHOTOGRAPHS SELECTED

Book layout → Final edits and last review → Book is published → Book available to readers in stores

MARKETING

Rick Riordan Today

Rick taught in San Francisco for eight years. After his children were born, he moved his family back to San Antonio. Rick continued teaching for a while but left his job after the Percy Jackson series was published. He no longer had the time to devote his attention to both of his careers. Rick decided to become a full-time writer. He has not left teaching entirely, however. Rick still likes to visit schools and talk to students about the writing process and his love of books. He hopes that, in doing so, he is encouraging children to read and write for their own enjoyment.

As a successful author, Rick has a demanding publishing schedule that includes not only writing, but **promoting** his books as well. He has to juggle his time between writing, making public appearances, and spending time with his family. His life is so busy that it takes Rick about one year to write each book.

🖋 Publishers often hold book launches to promote the release of a new title. When Rick's book *The Lost Hero* was released, the launch included a walking tree, people dressed as characters from the book, and chariot races.

One of Rick's favorite parts of being a children's author is meeting his fans. He has made appearances at schools, libraries, and bookstores all over the world. At these events, he is often greeted by hundreds of fans who are waiting for him to sign a copy of his book. Many of the fans come dressed as characters from Rick's books.

Rick loves seeing his readers become so involved in his stories. He continues to plan new books and series for his readers. Teaching readers about mythology through his writing remains one of Rick's main goals. He plans to introduce the myths of other peoples, including the Norse, into future books.

When attending promotional events for his books, Rick shares his love of reading with audience members and encourages them to become avid readers.

Writing About the Person Today

The biography of any living person is an ongoing story. People have new ideas, start new projects, and deal with challenges. For their work to be meaningful, biographers must include up-to-date information about their subjects. Through research, biographers try to answer the following questions.

1 Has the person received awards or recognition for accomplishments?

2 What is the person's life's work?

3 How have the person's accomplishments served others?

Fan Information

Rick is very appreciative of his fans. Thanks to them, Rick's books have become international bestsellers, selling millions of copies around the world. Part of this success can be attributed to Rick's relationship with his readers. He pays attention to their comments on his books and uses his readers' suggestions to create new stories and characters. When Rick's fans wanted more books about Percy Jackson, Rick created another series called Heroes of Olympus that brought back many of the characters in the Percy Jackson series.

Rick's website keeps fans up to date with Rick and the books he is working on.

Even though Rick loves interacting with his readers, he has had to reduce the number of public appearances he makes in a year. Attending events was taking him away from his family for long periods. His writing was suffering as well. Rick felt that it was important to devote more time to his family and to the books his fans want to read. Today, he only attends events that his publisher plans for him.

Rick uses his website to communicate with his fans. The site contains information about Rick and his books, along with a blog that provides updates on what Rick is reading and writing. If Rick is going to be visiting a bookstore or appearing on television, he makes sure that his site informs his fans of the date or location.

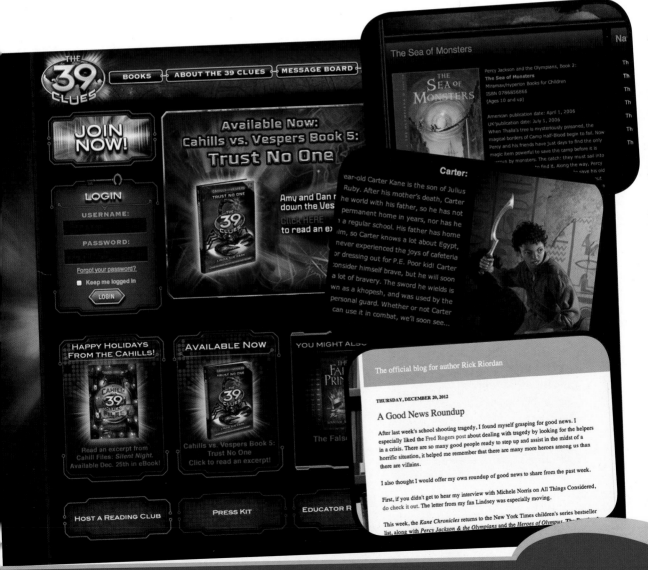

Write a Biography

A ll of the parts of a biography work together to tell the story of a person's life. Find out how these elements combine by writing a biography. Begin by choosing a person whose story fascinates you. You will have to research the person's life by using library books and reliable websites. You can also e-mail the person or write him or her a letter. The person might agree to answer your questions directly.

Use a concept web, such as the one below, to guide you in writing the biography. Answer each of the questions listed using the information you have gathered. Each heading on the concept web will form an important part of the person's story.

Parts of a Biography

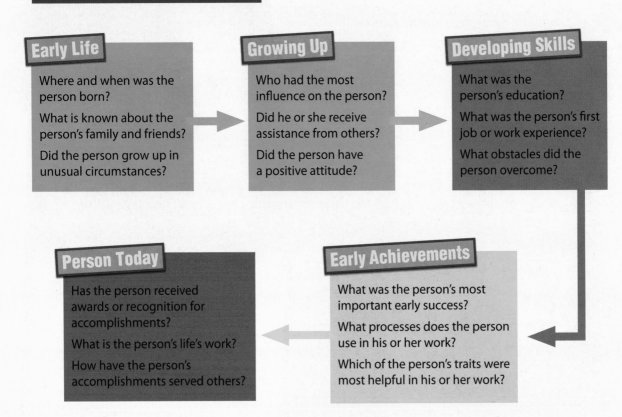

Early Life

Where and when was the person born?

What is known about the person's family and friends?

Did the person grow up in unusual circumstances?

Growing Up

Who had the most influence on the person?

Did he or she receive assistance from others?

Did the person have a positive attitude?

Developing Skills

What was the person's education?

What was the person's first job or work experience?

What obstacles did the person overcome?

Person Today

Has the person received awards or recognition for accomplishments?

What is the person's life's work?

How have the person's accomplishments served others?

Early Achievements

What was the person's most important early success?

What processes does the person use in his or her work?

Which of the person's traits were most helpful in his or her work?

Test Yourself

1 When and where was Rick Riordan born?

2 What middle grade teacher encouraged Rick to write?

3 How old was Rick when he submitted his first piece of writing for publication?

4 What did Rick first want to be when he was in college?

5 Which subjects did Rick study at the University of Texas at Austin?

6 What type of books did Rick first write and for whom?

7 What is the name of the summer camp Percy Jackson attends?

8 Which person in Rick's life inspired the character Percy Jackson?

9 Rick's books are based on the mythology of which ancient civilizations?

10 What is the name of the book series that Rick co-writes with other children's authors?

Writing Terms

The field of writing has its own language. Understanding some of the more common writing terms will allow you to discuss your ideas about books.

action: the moving events of a work of fiction

antagonist: the person in the story who opposes the main character

autobiography: a history of a person's life written by that person

biography: a written account of another person's life

character: a person in a story, poem, or play

climax: the most exciting moment or turning point in a story

episode: a scene or short piece of action in a story

fiction: stories about characters and events that are not real

foreshadow: hinting at something that is going to happen later in the book

imagery: a written description of a thing or idea that brings an image to mind

narrator: the speaker of the story who relates the events

nonfiction: writing that deals with real people and events

novel: published writing of considerable length that portrays characters within a story

plot: the order of events in a work of fiction

protagonist: the leading character of a story; often a likable character

resolution: the end of the story, when the conflict is settled

scene: a single episode in a story

setting: the place and time in which a work of fiction occurs

theme: an idea that runs throughout a work of fiction

Key Words

attention deficit hyperactivity disorder: a condition in which a person is unable to pay attention to a task for a steady period and is easily distracted

civilizations: social groups that have a distinctive cultural and economic organization

dedication: committed to a task or purpose

demigod: the offspring of a god and a mortal, who may have some supernatural powers

discipline: controlled behavior, or self-control

draft: a rough copy of a story

dyslexia: a condition that affects a person's ability to read, write, and spell

Egyptologist: someone who studies the culture and artifacts of ancient Egypt

folktales: stories told orally amongst a group of people

genre: a category or group of art or literature

Golden Fleece: from Greek mythology, the hair of a winged ram that was stolen from the king of Colchis

graphic design: designing or electronic forms of visual information

literature: writing of lasting value, including plays, poems, and novels

manuscript: a draft of a story before it is published

Medieval: a period of European History dating from the 5th to the 15th century

mythology: stories about supernatural creatures

nominated: entered as a candidate for an award

Norse: Scandinavian people

professional: doing a job to earn a living

promoting: advertising a product for the purpose of selling

revised: changed something to make it better

sequel: a story that is related to a previous story

short stories: works of fiction that are usually less than 10,000 words

University Interscholastic League: an organization created by The University of Texas at Austin to provide extracurricular activities

vocational: of or relating to an occupation or job

Index

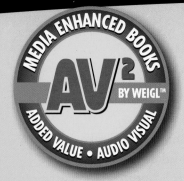

Log on to www.av2books.com

AV² by Weigl brings you media enhanced books that support active learning. Go to www.av2books.com, and enter the special code found on page 2 of this book. You will gain access to enriched and enhanced content that supplements and complements this book. Content includes video, audio, weblinks, quizzes, a slide show, and activities.

AV² Online Navigation

Audio
Listen to sections of the book read aloud.

Book Pages
AV² pages directly correspond to pages in the book.

Video
Watch informative video clips.

Key Words
Study vocabulary, and complete a matching word activity.

Embedded Weblinks
Gain additional information for research.

Try This!
Complete activities and hands-on experiments.

Quizzes
Test your knowledge.

Slide Show
View images and captions, and prepare a presentation.

AV² was built to bridge the gap between print and digital. We encourage you to tell us what you like and what you want to see in the future.

Sign up to be an AV² Ambassador at www.av2books.com/ambassador.